R. BERNAL

All Smiles

Senior Authors

Roger C. Farr

Dorothy S. Strickland

Authors

Richard F. Abrahamson ◆ Alma Flor Ada ◆ Barbara Bowen Coulter
Bernice E. Cullinan ◆ Margaret A. Gallego
W. Dorsey Hammond
Nancy Roser ◆ Junko Yokota ◆ Hallie Kay Yopp

Senior Consultant

Asa G. Hilliard III

Consultants

V. Kanani Choy ◆ Lee Bennett Hopkins ◆ Stephen Krashen ◆ Rosalia Salinas

Harcourt Brace & Company

Orlando Atlanta Austin Boston San Francisco Chicago Dallas New York Toronto London

All rights reserved. No part of this publication may be reproduced or transmitted in any form or by any means, electronic or mechanical, including photocopy, recording, or any information storage and retrieval system, without permission in writing from the publisher.

Requests for permission to make copies of any part of the work should be mailed to: Permissions Department, Harcourt Brace & Company, 6277 Sea Harbor Drive, Orlando, Florida 32887-6777.

HARCOURT BRACE and Quill Design is a registered trademark of Harcourt Brace & Company.

Acknowledgments appear in the back of this work.

Printed in the United States of America

ISBN 0-15-307865-0

4 5 6 7 8 9 10   048   99 98 97

Dear Reader,

You can visit many places when you read. In **All Smiles**, you will blast off into space and see the planets. Back on earth, you will go to a beautiful land in South America and meet a girl named Silvia. A pig from Alaska will greet you when you visit Maya's house.

Every story is a doorway that opens into a new world. Open the door, come in, and smile!

Sincerely,

The Authors

The Authors

Pets Are Special Animals

4

Contents

Beyond My World

CONTENTS

Family News

Contents

Pets Are Special Animals

One pet, two pets — **old pets, new pets.**

Meet a cat who gets into trouble and a dog who hates baths.

Then take a close look at some **real pets.**

Maybe you will meet a

favorite **pet** as you read these stories.

Contents

Bookshelf

The next day Alfie caught a bullfrog in the pond. "You can have him for a pet," he told Laura. But Laura wouldn't look at it.

...d Susan said Laura
...her water snake,
...creamed and ran
...ouse.

Furry

by Holly Keller

At last Laura finds the **perfect pet.**

What could it be?

Award-Winning Author
SIGNATURES LIBRARY

Pet Show
by Ezra Jack Keats

Archie wants his cat to be in a **pet show,** but his cat is not around. So he takes a new kind of pet and wins!

Award-Winning Author

See How They Grow: Kitten
by Jan Burton

Follow a **kitten** as it grows up and learns about the world.

Millions of Cats
by Wanda Gag

Read to find out what happens when some **pet owners** find "millions and billions and trillions of cats."

Lewis Carroll Shelf Award

Dreams

EZRA JACK KEATS

It was hot.
After supper Roberto came
to his window to talk with Amy.
"Look what I made in school today—
a paper mouse!"
"Does it do anything?" Amy asked.
Roberto thought for a while.
"I don't know," he said. Then he put
the mouse on the windowsill.

15

As it grew darker, the city got quieter.
"Bedtime, Roberto," called his mother.
"Bedtime for you, too,"
other mothers called.
"Good-night, Amy."
"Good-night, Roberto."
"G-o-o-o-o-d-night!" echoed the parrot.
Soon they were all in bed.

17

Someone began to dream.
Soon everybody was dreaming—
except one person.
Somehow Roberto just couldn't fall asleep.
It got later and later.

Finally he got up
and went to the window.
What he saw down in the street
made him gasp!
There was Archie's cat!
A big dog had chased him into a box.
The dog snarled.
"He's trapped!" thought Roberto.
"What should I do?"

Then it happened!
His pajama sleeve
brushed the paper mouse
off the windowsill.
It sailed away from him.

Down it fell,
turning this way
and that,
casting a big shadow
on the wall.

The shadow grew bigger—
and bigger—

23

and BIGGER!
The dog howled and ran away.
The cat dashed across the street
and jumped through Archie's open window.
"Wow! Wait till I tell Archie what happened!"
thought Roberto.
"That was some mouse!"
He yawned and went back to bed.

Morning came, and everybody
was getting up.
Except one person.

Roberto was fast asleep,
dreaming.

Ezra Jack Keats

Ezra Jack Keats

Ezra Jack Keats loved to draw. Once, when he was very young, he drew pictures all over a table. His mother didn't even get mad. She just said, "Now isn't that nice!" and showed the table to all her friends.

When he grew up, Ezra Jack Keats loved children. "I am an ex-kid," he would say. The children he drew in his books seemed real to him. He said they gave him story ideas. Which characters in *Dreams* seemed real to you?

Response Corner

Make Paper Animals

"Dreams" is a story about how Roberto's
paper mouse saves a cat. You can make
a paper animal and write a story about it, too.

You will need:
a tracer • a sheet of paper • scissors • glue • crayons

1. Fold a sheet of paper in half.

2. On the open side, trace the half circle.

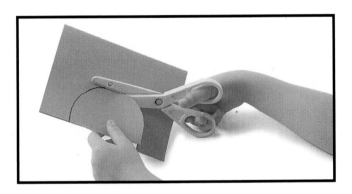

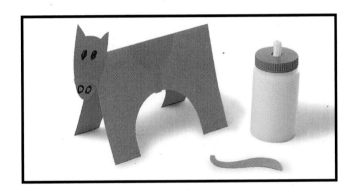

3. Cut on the line.

4. Make the head and tail and glue them on.

After you write your story you can

- share your story.
- put your paper animals with the others. Tell or write stories about them.

What Do You Think?

Pretend that Roberto's paper mouse could talk.
What would it say about what happened?

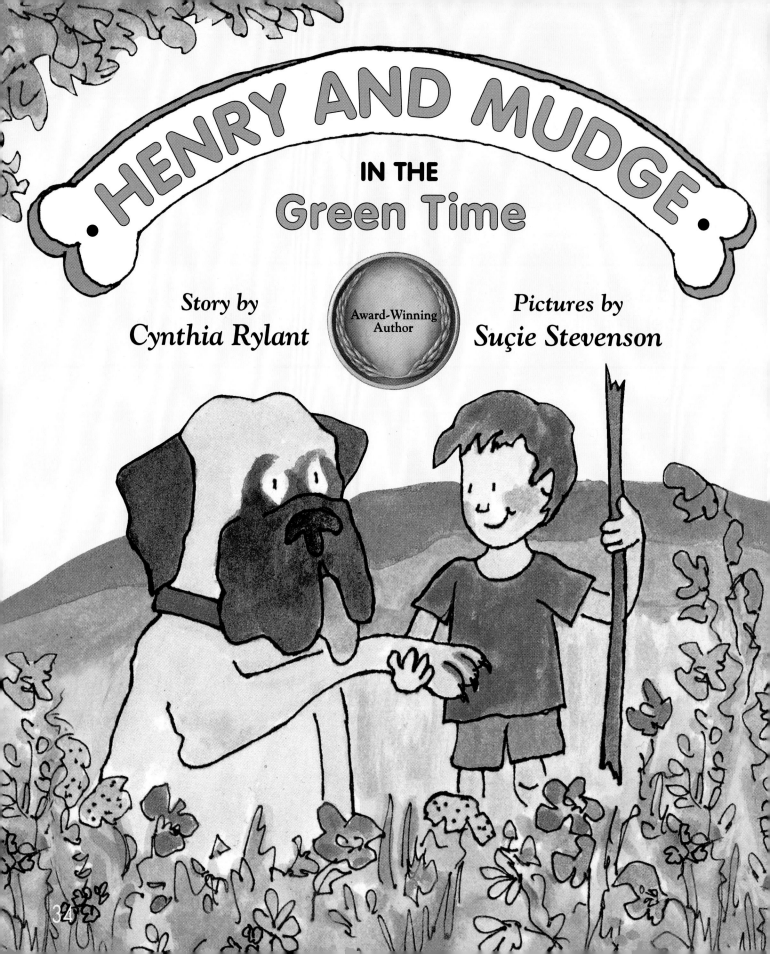

HENRY AND MUDGE

IN THE
Green Time

Story by
Cynthia Rylant

Award-Winning
Author

Pictures by
Suçie Stevenson

The Bath

On hot days Henry liked
to give Mudge a bath.
Henry liked it
because he could
play with the water hose and
because he could cool off.

Mudge hated it.
Mudge knew when
he was going to get
a bath.

He would see Henry
looking for the dog shampoo.

And when he saw Henry hooking up
the water hose,
he tried to hide
under the steps.

But it never worked.

Henry would take Mudge
into the front yard
in the sun, and he would
hose him down.

Mudge hated it.
His eyes drooped,
his ears drooped,
and his tail drooped.

When he was all wet,

he looked like a big walrus.

Henry laughed at him.

Then Henry would soap him up.

Henry scrubbed his head

and his neck

and his back

and his chest

and his stomach

and his legs

and his tail.

Mudge really hated

this part.

He drooped even more.

Then Henry
hosed Mudge down again.

But before Henry
could grab a towel,
before Henry could get Mudge dry,
Mudge always got Henry back.
Because when Henry
let go—

Mudge started shaking.
He started with his head,
then he shook his neck
and his back

44

and his chest
and his stomach
and his legs
and his tail.

Mudge shook so hard
that when he was done,
he was mostly dry,
and Henry was mostly wet.

Then Mudge looked at Henry
and wagged his tail
while Henry
dried Henry
with the towel.

Cynthia Rylant

Cynthia Rylant grew up in the country. It was hard to get books since she lived so far from town. She and her best friend often made up their own stories.

When Cynthia Rylant grew up, she worked in a library. She says, "I fell in love with children's books in the library. It was there that I decided to spend my life writing them."

Some of this writer's story ideas come from her own life. Henry and Mudge are like her son, Nate, and a big dog named Mudge. She says the real Mudge hates baths, too!

♡ Cynthia Rylant

Suçie Stevenson

Suçie Stevenson really knows how to give a big dog a bath. She has two big dogs of her own.

The artist started drawing when she was very young. Every time one of her brothers or sisters had a birthday, she made a funny card. She has five brothers and three sisters, so she got a lot of practice!

Suçie Stevenson and her dogs live near the seashore. Her favorite thing to do is to take walks on the beach—even in the rain!

Suçie
Stevenson

49

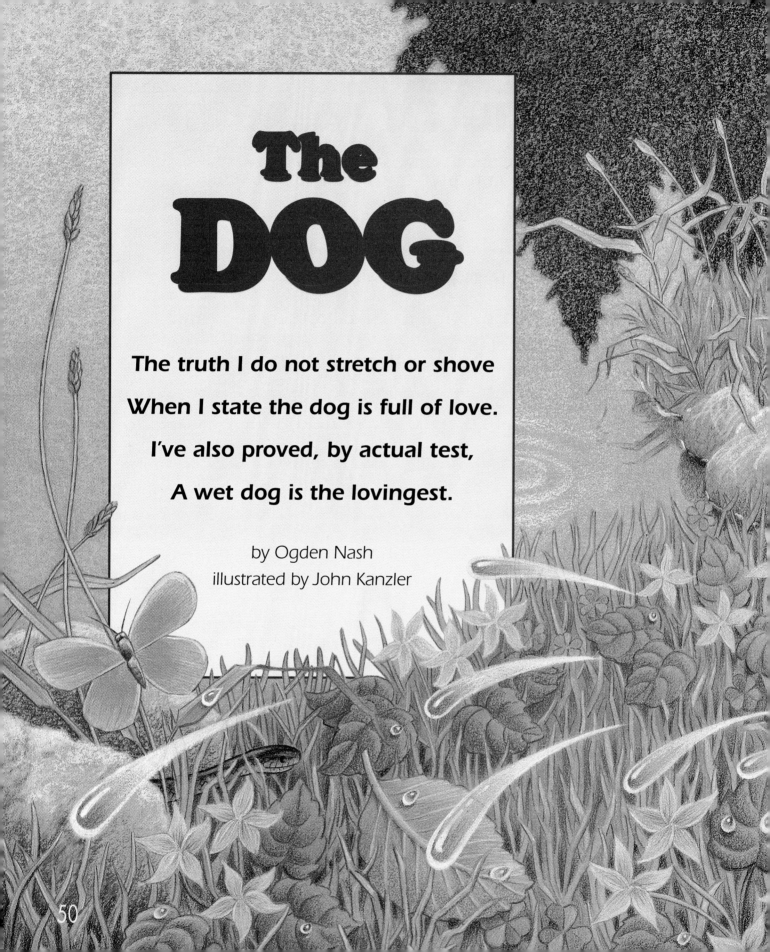

The DOG

The truth I do not stretch or shove

When I state the dog is full of love.

I've also proved, by actual test,

A wet dog is the lovingest.

by Ogden Nash
illustrated by John Kanzler

50

Response Corner

Make a Mudge Mask

Wouldn't it be fun to act out the Henry and Mudge story you just read? You can make a Mudge Mask from a paper bag. Then you can put on a play about Henry and Mudge.

YOU WILL NEED

Big paper bag • Colored Paper

Scissors • Crayons

White Glue

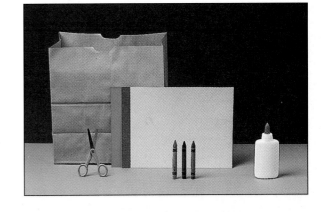

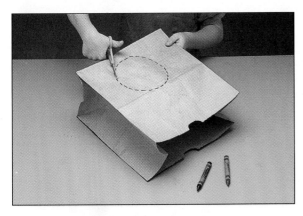

1. Cut a hole for your face.

2. Cut an arm hole on each side.

3. Make ears and a tongue.
   Glue them on.

4. Add a dog collar.
   Add some other things.

What Do You Think?

How did Mudge feel before his bath? How did he feel after?

Pets

MICHAEL DUNNING

Dog

puppy

Dogs need to be taken
for walks outdoors.
They like to chase after
balls and sticks.
A young dog is called
a puppy. All dogs bark
and wag their tails
when they're excited.

paw

56

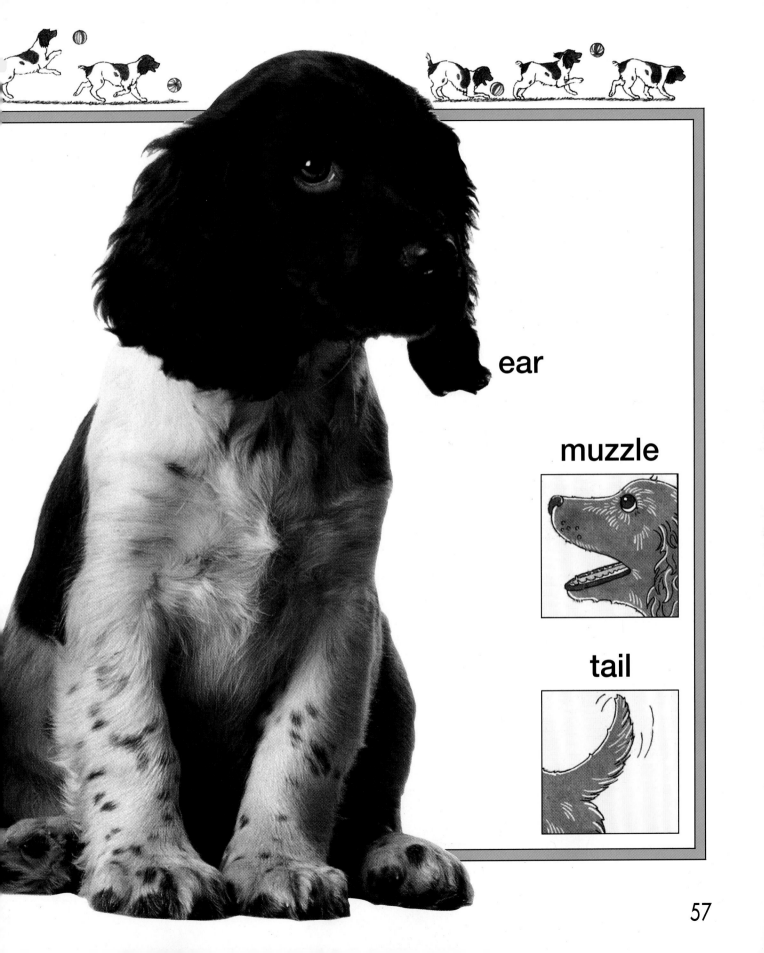

ear

muzzle

tail

57

Parakeet

A parakeet is a colorful bird that chirps. It lives in a cage. Parakeets use their sharp beaks to crack open seeds.

tail

beak

feathers

claws

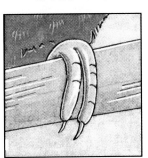

Cat

Cats have soft fur and like to be petted.

They purr when they are happy.

A young cat is called a kitten. Kittens love to play and pounce. All cats sleep a lot during the day. They hunt mice at night.

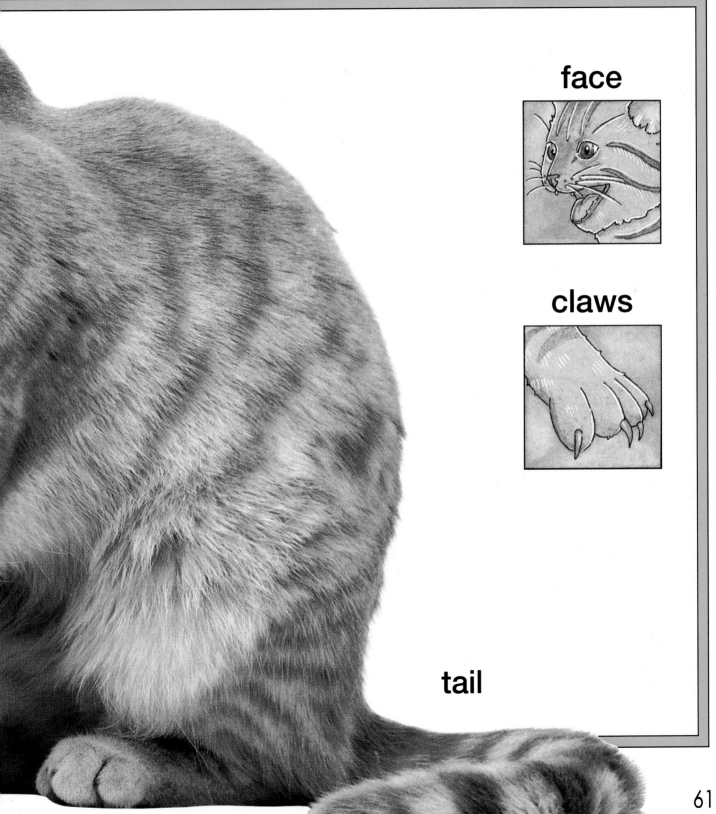

face

claws

tail

Guinea pig

Guinea pigs are greedy about food. They grow fat if they do not get enough exercise. Guinea pigs can be very shy. They like to hide away from people in a nest of warm woodchips.

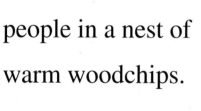

nose

paw ear

Rabbit

Rabbits hear very well with their big ears. They can run fast to escape from danger. Pet rabbits live in hutches. They like to eat carrots and fresh greens. Rabbits use their paws to dig holes in the ground.

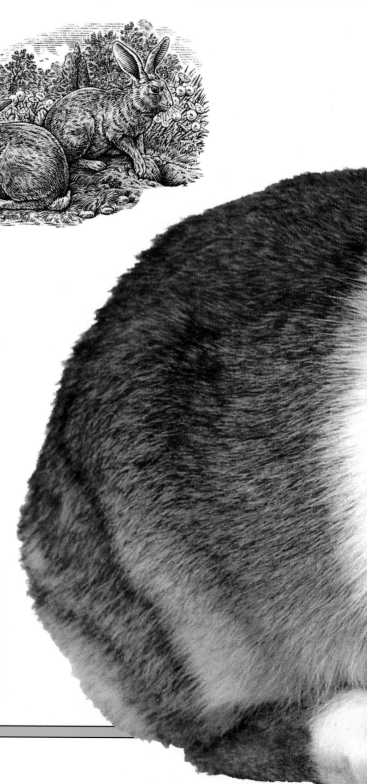

paw

tail

ear

nose

Goldfish

Goldfish live in fish
tanks. Their bodies
are covered in bright,
shiny scales. A goldfish uses
its fins and tail to swim through
the water. Goldfish must be fed
special fish food every day.

tail

fin

gills

scales

67

Hamster

Hamsters have pockets in their cheeks that they use to collect seeds. They also gather seeds and store them in their cages to eat when they get hungry. Hamsters have sharp front teeth for gnawing their food.

ear

teeth

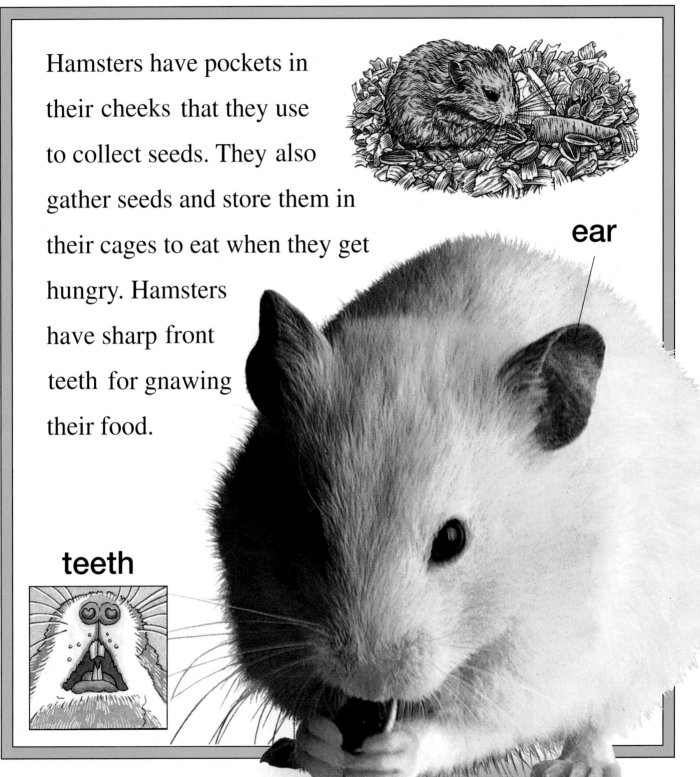

Photographer

Talking with
Michael Dunning

Do you have any pets?

I have a ginger cat named Basil. Her picture is not in the book, though.

How did you take pictures of the pets in this book?

The animals were brought into the studio one at a time. Then I followed them around and took pictures. It was fun. Only the very best pictures made it into the book.

How can children take good pictures of their pets?

Take your pet out on a bright, sunny day. As you follow it around, get really close so the pet is the main thing in the picture.

Pet Peek-Over Bookmarks

In "Pets" you read about many pets.
Here's a way to make a bookmark with
your favorite pet peeking over the top.
You can write inside what you know
about that pet.

70

1. Fold a half sheet of paper in half.

2. Make the pet's face and glue it to the top.

3. Open the bookmark and write what you know about the pet inside.

After you make your bookmark, you can read it to a classmate.

What Do You Think?

If you could own a pet, which one would you choose? Why?

71

THEME

Beyond My World

Blast off to another planet with Snail.
Visit the planets and see a space city.
Jump into your spaceship and buckle up!

CONTENTS

Bookshelf

a ball of rock with neither air nor water—so people and animals and plants can't live there.

Rookie Read-About™ Science

So That's How the Moon Changes Shape!

By Allan Fowler

14

15

So That's How the Moon Changes Shape!
by Allan Fowler

Does the moon really change its shape?
Find out by reading this book.

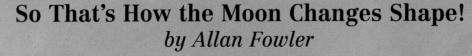

Signatures Library

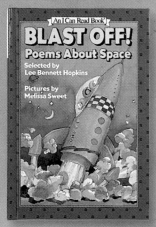

Blast Off! Poems about Space
selected by Lee Bennett Hopkins

Here is a book of poems about the shiny moon, bright stars, and other things in space!

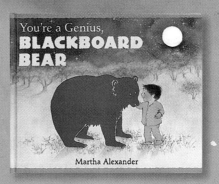

You're a Genius, Blackboard Bear
by Martha Alexander

A boy wants to go into space. Can Blackboard Bear help him get his wish?

Award-Winning Author

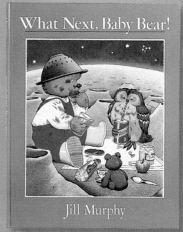

What Next, Baby Bear!
by Jill Murphy

Join Baby Bear as he blasts off to the moon.

Award-Winning Author

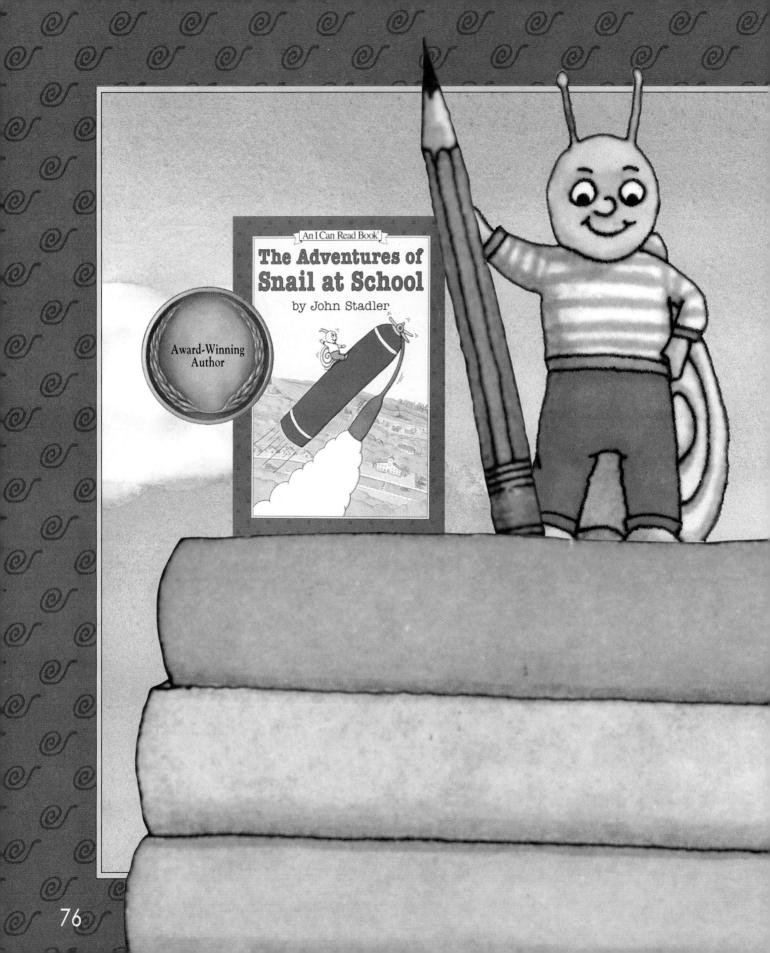

The Adventures of Snail at School

by John Stadler

The New Student

"Class, we will have a new student today," said Mrs. Harvey.

"Will someone pick her up from the principal's office?"

"I can do it," said Snail.

"Well, all right, Snail," said Mrs. Harvey.

"But please hurry."

"I will be back in a flash," said Snail.

Snail hurried down the long hallway.
"I will show Mrs. Harvey she can
count on me," he said.
Snail came to the principal's office.
There was a fire extinguisher by the door.
"This should not be here," he said.
"I will put it back."

Snail pushed.

Suddenly he heard

Hisssss!

He grabbed the fire extinguisher.

It started to shake, rattle, and roll.

"Yikes!" Snail cried.

"It's blasting off!"

"Look at me!
I am in outer space,"
Snail shouted.

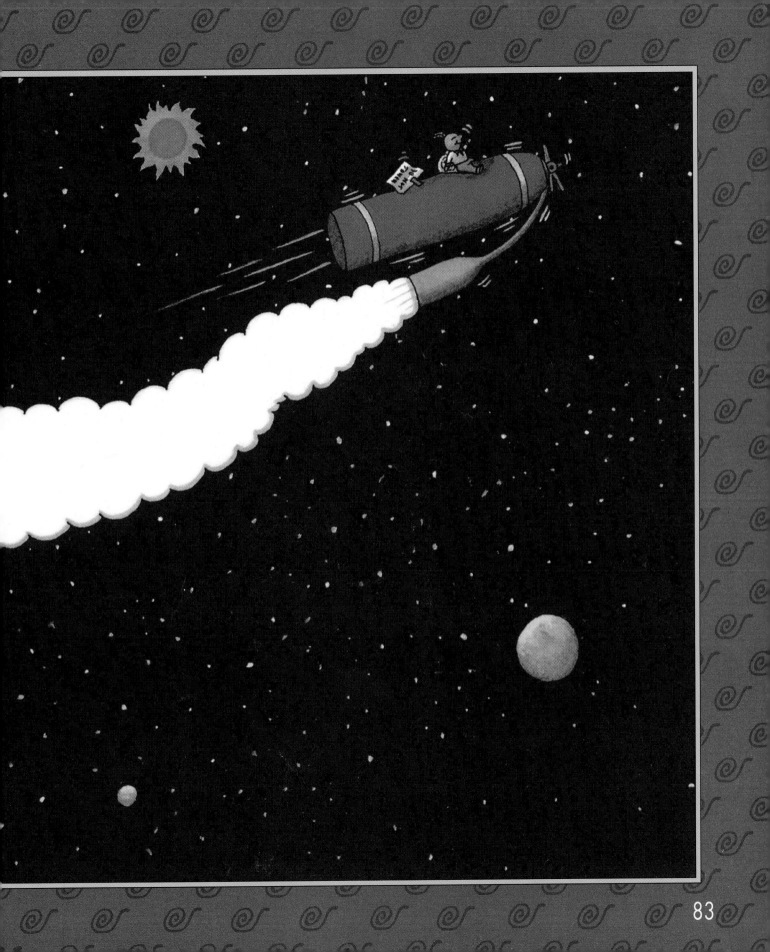

Snail landed on another planet.
"Is anybody home?" Snail called.
Suddenly he saw something move.
"Monsters!" cried Snail.

Then he looked closer.

"You are not monsters," said Snail.

"You look like me!"

"Welcome to our planet," said one of them.

"My name is Edie."

"Come and join our party," said Edie.

"Nice cake," said Snail.

"Have a piece," said Edie.

"Thank you very much," Snail said,
"but I must get back to my classroom."

"I can take you
in our rocket,"
said Edie.
"Great!" said Snail.
Edie and Snail
took off for Earth.

"This is my school," said Snail.

"We must hurry.

Mrs. Harvey is waiting for us."

"Snail, where have you been?" asked Mrs. Harvey. "You could have gone around the world in the time you were away!"

"Well," said Snail, "the fire extinguisher took off, and I went into space and . . ."

"Now, Snail, please sit down," Mrs. Harvey said, "and stop making up stories."

Mrs. Harvey looked at Edie.

"You must be the new student," she said.

"Her name is Edie," said Snail.

"She comes from another planet."

"That is enough, Snail," said Mrs. Harvey.

"Welcome to the class, Edie. You may take your seat next to Snail."

Then Mrs. Harvey looked closer.

"Edie is floating!" she said to herself.

"Snail?" Mrs. Harvey asked.

"Yes, Mrs. Harvey," said Snail.

"Oh, never mind, Snail," said Mrs. Harvey.

"Never mind."

A letter from . . .
John Stadler

Dear Boys and Girls,

　　When I was in school, everything around me seemed so big and interesting. Whenever I was alone in the hallway, while the other children were in class, I was very excited. The halls were very quiet, and things like fire extinguishers caught my eye. These memories helped me think of the stories in *The Adventures of Snail at School.* Maybe something you see in the school hallway will make you think of an exciting story.

Your friend,

John Stadler

RESPONSE CORNER

AN INTERVIEW WITH
Snail and Edie

Pretend that Edie and Snail came to visit
your class. What would you like to ask
them about their trip into space?
You can be a news reporter
and ask Edie and Snail
questions.

Questions
1. Snail, how did it feel
to ride on a fire
extinguisher?
2. Edie, why were you
having a party?
3. Snail, what did you
like best about
Edie's planet?

Edie

Make a microphone like the one you see. Write some questions to ask Snail and Edie. Take turns being the reporter and being Snail and Edie.

After you practice, you can
- pretend you are on TV as you talk to Snail and Edie.
- talk to Snail's teacher and the children in Snail's class.

What Do You Think?
Would you like to have Edie as a new student in your class? Why or why not?

Snail

BY Tim Wood   ILLUSTRATED BY Tony Wells

OUT IN SPACE

Would you like to live out in space? One day people may get the chance.

People will probably live in a giant spinning space city shaped like a wheel. There might be lots of homes inside the wheel.

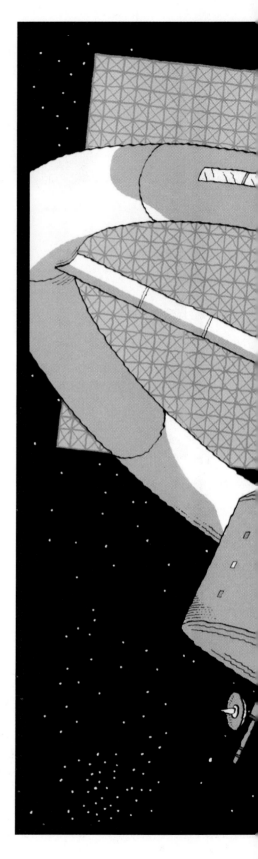

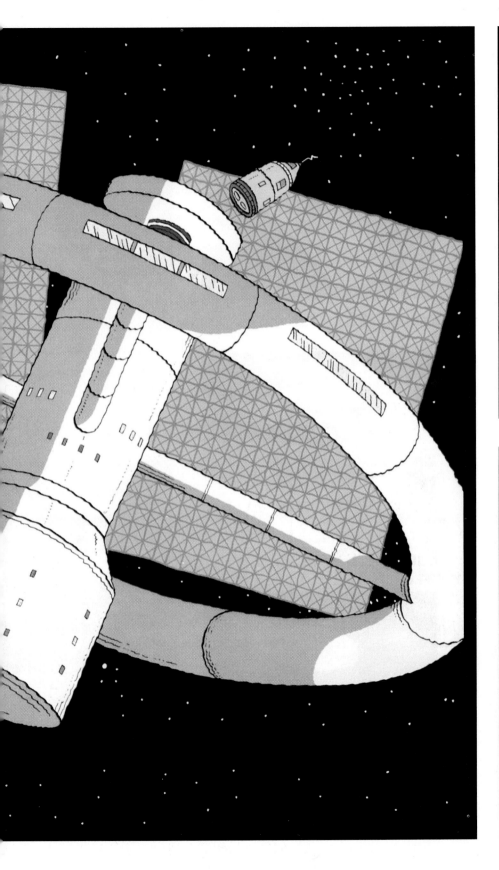

Homes might be round with no flat walls for hanging pictures.

Huge panels outside would catch sunlight to make power for lights and machines.

People would grow their food in greenhouses.

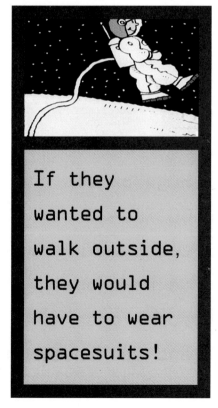

If they wanted to walk outside, they would have to wear spacesuits!

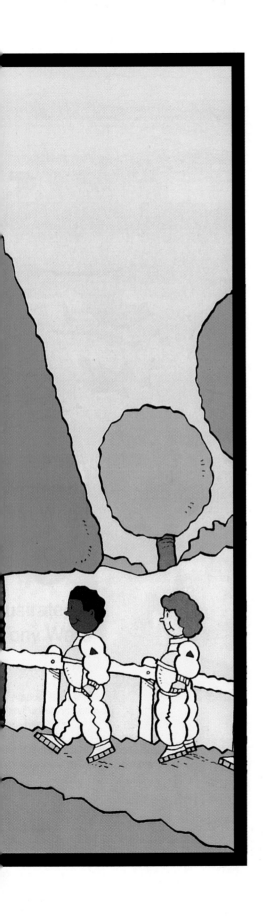

Would you like to live in a space city?

Maybe someday you will.

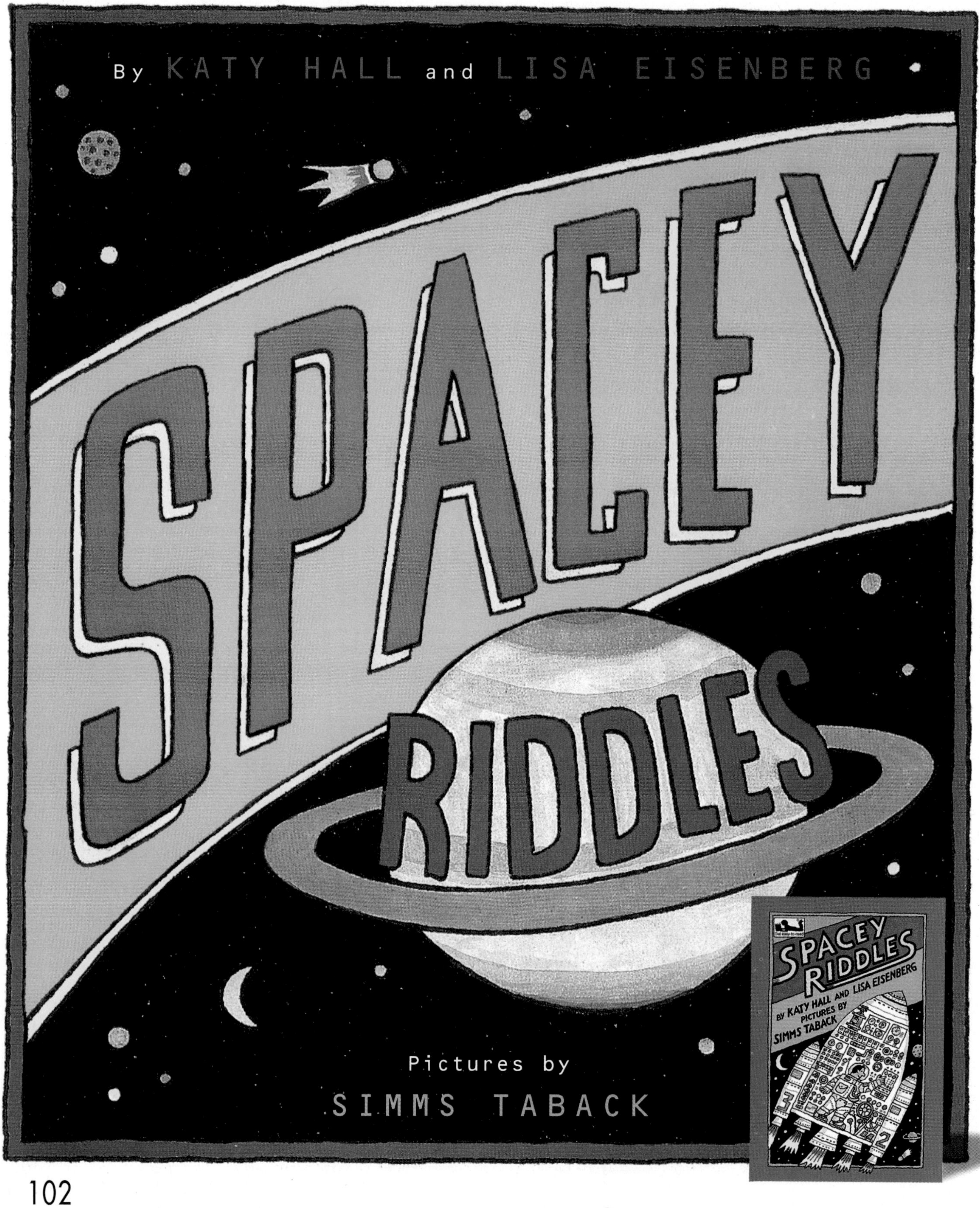

By KATY HALL and LISA EISENBERG
SPACEY
RIDDLES
Pictures by
SIMMS TABACK
SPACEY
RIDDLES
BY KATY HALL AND LISA EISENBERG
PICTURES BY
SIMMS TABACK

What is
the astronaut's
favorite meal?

Launch!

How would you
recognize an
elephant on
the moon?

By the big
E on its
space suit!

What kind
of songs
do planets like
to sing?

Neptunes!

Why did the
astronaut take
a nap so close
to the sun?

She was
a light sleeper!

And how did the astronaut serve drinks?

In sun glasses!

What's soft and white and comes from Mars?

A Mars-mallow!

Written by **Kim Jackson**

Our world is
a planet
named **Earth**.

Nine planets
move around
the sun.

Our **sun**
is not a planet.
It is a **star!**
Our sun gives us
heat and **light**.

Planets close
to the sun are
very hot.

Planets far
from the sun are
very cold.

113

A planet named **Mercury** is **closest** to the sun. Mercury is **very hot**!

A planet named **Venus** looks bright. From Earth, Venus looks **bright**, like a star!

A planet
named **Mars**
is **red**.
Mars has
two moons!

A planet named **Jupiter** is very **big**. Jupiter is the **biggest** planet.

A planet named **Saturn** has **rings**. The rings are made of **ice** and **rock**.

A planet
named **Uranus**
also has **rings**.
Uranus has rings
and **moons**!

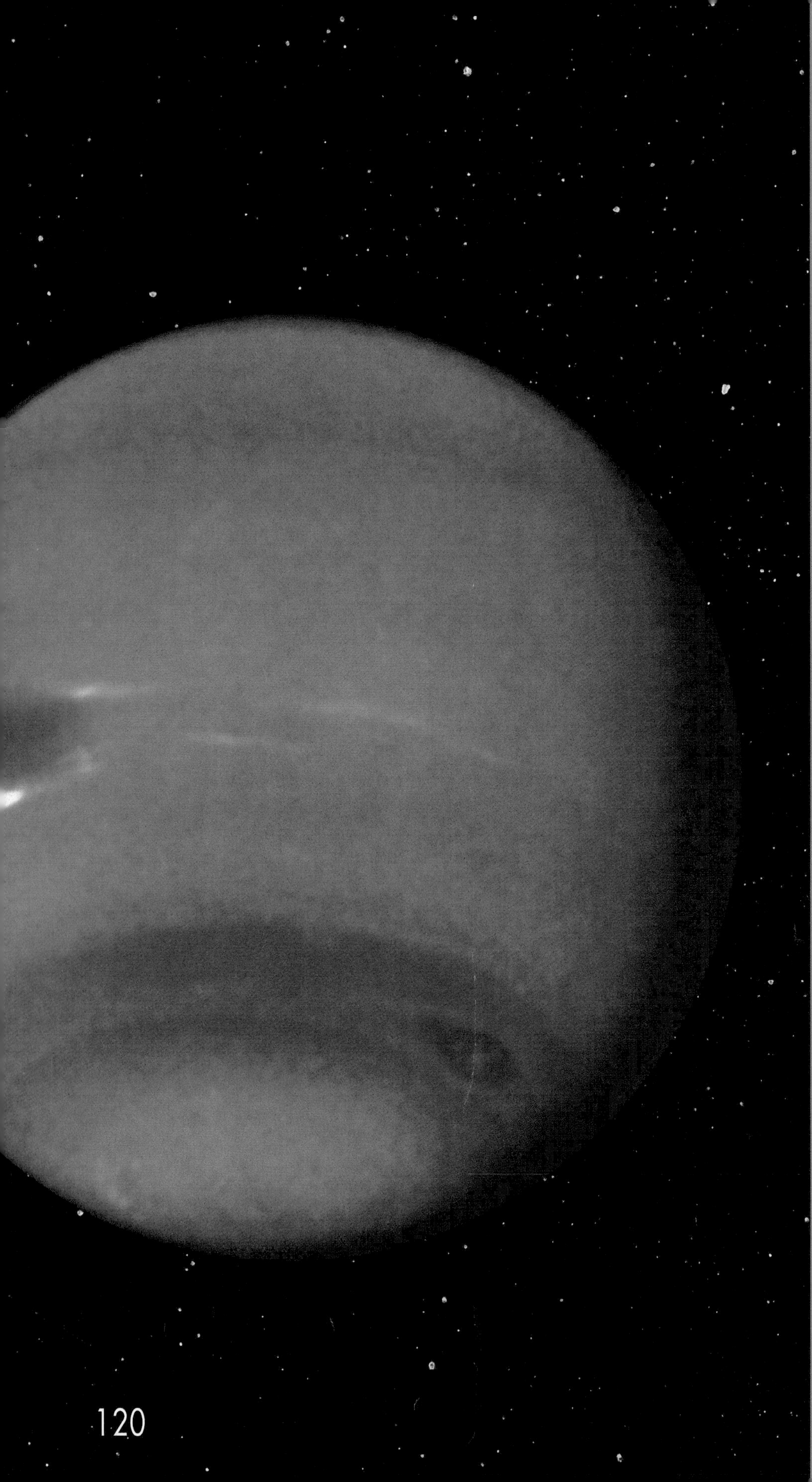

A planet
named
Neptune
is **far** away.
Neptune is
almost **too far**
for us to see.

A planet named **Pluto** is **very far** from the sun. It is very **cold** there! Pluto has one moon.

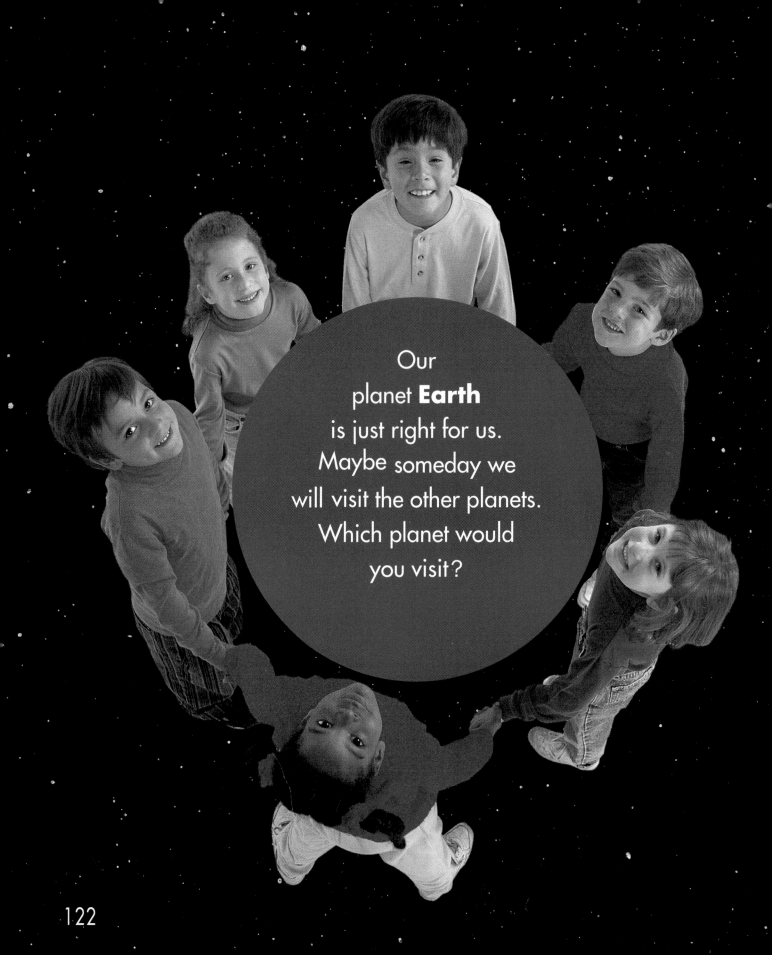

Our
planet **Earth**
is just right for us.
Maybe someday we
will visit the other planets.
Which planet would
you visit?

About the Photographs

The *Voyager* took many of the pictures in "Planets." This spacecraft was sent into space on a rocket. First, it took pictures of Earth. Then, it flew far from home. It took pictures of planets, stars, and other space objects.

Now, the Hubble telescope is in space. It takes pictures of objects in space that are very far away. What do you think this "eye in the sky" might see?

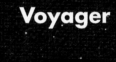

Voyager

Hubble telescope

Always quiet,
Always blinking,
By day sleeping,
At night winking.

The Stars

Siempre quietas,
Siempre inquietas,
Durmiendo de día,
De noche despiertas.

Las estrellas

By Nelly Palacio Jaramillo

Vincent van Gogh
1853–1890
Starry Night over the Rhone River
Musee d'Orsay, Paris, France

Why

We zoomed
to the moon
in just
a few years.

Why can't
we grow
onions
and
leave
out
the tears?

by
Prince Redcloud

illustrated by
Peggy Tagel

127

RESPONSE CORNER

My Very Own Planet

What would happen if you found a new planet?
What would it look like?
What would you name it?
You can make your own planet
and write about it.

You will need:

brushes

paper circles

paints

PAINT

glue

GLUE

scissors

glitter

I found a planet. I named it Glow. The sky is green and the grass is blue.

128

1. Paint and decorate your planet.

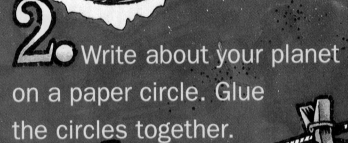

2. Write about your planet on a paper circle. Glue the circles together.

My planet is Twinkle. It is made of ice. It is too cold to live there.

After you make your planet, you can be a tour guide and show the planets to classmates.
• Write a guide that tells about all the planets.

What Do You Think?

What was the most interesting thing you learned about the nine planets?

THEME

Family News

CONTENTS

Families everywhere grow and change.

Find out what's new in each of the families in these stories.

Would you like a new baby brother, a pet pig, or some brand-new shoes?

Visit these families and see the changes that happen.

Bookshelf

PABLO'S TREE *by Pat Mora*

On the day Pablo was adopted, his grandfather planted a little tree. Every year on that day, his grandfather hangs something new on the tree.

Award-Winning Author
SIGNATURES LIBRARY

D.W. ALL WET
by Marc Brown

D.W. will not go in the water
when she goes to the beach.
Then her brother has an idea.

Award-Winning Author/Illustrator

WHEN I AM OLD WITH YOU
by Angela Johnson

A girl tells her granddaddy
about all the wonderful things
they will do when they are
old together.

ALA Notable Book

A MOTHER FOR CHOCO
by Keiko Kasza

A little bird named
Choco goes to look for his
mother. Where could she be?

Award-Winning Author

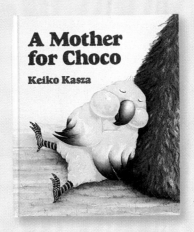

Geraldine's Baby Brother

Baby Brother

HOLLY KELLER

Geraldine put on her earmuffs
and sat behind the big chair.
"Why are you wearing earmuffs in the house?"
Uncle Albert asked when he saw her.
"So I can't hear *it*," Geraldine snapped, and
she pointed to Willie's basket.

"But I thought you wanted
a baby brother,"
Uncle Albert said.
"Not *that* one," Geraldine
grumbled, and she
turned the page without
looking up.

The doorbell rang and
Willie started to cry.
Mama came out of
the kitchen.

Aunt Bessie came down from the bedroom, and Papa got up from the sofa.

It was Mrs. Wilson to see Mama. She had a big present for Willie and a present for Geraldine, too.

"And where *is* Geraldine?" Mrs. Wilson asked while she was tickling Willie.

"Nowhere," Geraldine snarled from behind the chair.

So Mrs. Wilson left Geraldine's present on the table.

Willie cried all morning.
Aunt Bessie picked him up
and patted him.

Mama gave him a bottle,
and Papa carried him
all around the house.

Uncle Albert made funny faces. But at lunchtime Willie was still crying. "Oh, dear," Mama said suddenly. "Where's Geraldine? She must be starving."

Geraldine was in her room.

"How about a sandwich?" asked Mama.

Geraldine turned away. "I don't see you."

Mama sat down on the edge of the bed, but Geraldine slid off the other side and walked out the door.

Late in the afternoon Geraldine came into the kitchen. "I'm going to take my bath now, and then I'm going to bed."

"That's nice, dear," Mama said quickly over her shoulder. Willie was still screaming.

Papa was waiting outside the bathroom
when Geraldine opened the door.
"Aunt Bessie made lasagna for dinner,
Geraldine, especially for you."
"Not hungry," Geraldine grumbled, and she
disappeared into her room.

In the middle of the night Geraldine heard Willie moving around in his basket. She got out of bed and marched across the hall to the nursery.

"No more crying," she said sternly. Willie looked at her and yawned. "I mean it," she added.

Willie rubbed his face
and stuck out his tongue.
"You're weird," she said.

Willie stuffed his hand
into his mouth and
sneezed, and Geraldine
laughed because she
couldn't help it.
But Willie didn't cry.
Geraldine stuck her
fingers in her ears,
and he still didn't cry.

She turned on the light, and Willie gurgled. So she sat in the rocking chair and read him some stories.

In the morning Mama found them both asleep. "Breakfast, anyone?" she whispered. Geraldine opened her eyes. She was *really* hungry. "Can I give Willie his bottle?" she asked, and she patted Willie's head.

"How nice," Mama said. "Can I give you a hug?"

"Soon," Geraldine answered, and she went
downstairs for breakfast.

• Holly Keller •

You have written many stories about Geraldine. Is Geraldine like anyone you know?

Geraldine is a blend of my daughter and me. Like my daughter, Geraldine has to have the last word. Once, my daughter dressed herself in funny-looking school clothes. I told her, "You look silly in those clothes." My daughter said, "So then don't look at me!"

My daughter is now 24 years old, and she loves Geraldine. Geraldine is her favorite heroine.

Holly Keller

I am the sister of him
        And he is my brother.
He is too little for us
        To talk to each other.

So every morning I show him
        My doll and my book;
But every morning he still is
        Too little to look.

by Dorothy Aldis
illustrated by Rita Lascaro

151

Response Corner

Geraldine's Family Album

Think about all the fun Geraldine will have with her brother as he gets older. You can make a family album with pictures of Geraldine and her brother doing things together.

Draw a picture of Geraldine and her brother doing something.

Then **write** a sentence about your picture on a paper strip.

Glue your picture and paper strip in Geraldine's family album.

Geraldine and her brother rake leaves.

Geraldine and her brother fly a kite.

Your class can read more books about Geraldine and add more pictures to the family album.

WHAT DO YOU THINK?
What problem was Geraldine having at the beginning of the story? What did she do about it?

Julius

STORY BY Angela Johnson

PICTURES BY Dav Pilkey

ALA Notable
Book
SLJ Best Books

JULIUS

BY ANGELA JOHNSON
S BY DAV PILKEY

Maya's granddaddy lived in Alabama, but wintered in Alaska.

He told Maya that was the reason he liked ice cubes in his coffee.

On one of Granddaddy's visits from Alaska, he brought a crate.

A surprise for Maya!

"Something that will teach you
fun and sharing." Granddaddy smiled.
"Something for my special you."
Maya hoped it was a horse or an older brother.
She'd always wanted one or the other.

HANDLE
WITH
CARE

But it was a pig.

A big pig.

An Alaskan pig, who did a polar bear imitation and climbed out of the crate.

Julius had come.

Maya's parents didn't think that they would like Julius.

He showed them no fun, no sharing.

Maya loved Julius, though, so he stayed.

159

There never was enough food in the house after Julius came to stay.

He slurped coffee and ate too much peanut butter.

He would roll himself in flour when
he wanted Maya to bake him cookies.

Julius made big messes and spread
the newspaper everywhere before anyone
could read it.

He left crumbs on the sheets and never
picked up his towels.

Julius made too much noise.

He'd stay up late watching old movies,
and he'd always play records when everybody
else wanted to read.

But Maya knew the other Julius too. . . .
The Julius who was fun to take on walks
'cause he did great dog imitations and chased cats.
The Julius who sneaked into stores
with her and tried on clothes.
Julius liked anything blue and stretchy.

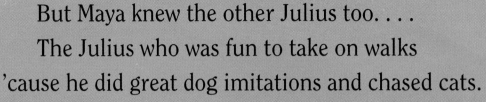

They'd try on hats too.

Maya liked red felt.

Julius liked straw—it tasted better.

Trying on shoes was hard, though. . . .

Julius would swing for hours
on the playground with Maya.

He'd protect her from the scary
things at night too . . . sometimes.

Maya loved the Julius who taught her how to dance to jazz records . . . and eat peanut butter from the jar, without getting any on the ceiling.

Maya didn't think all the older brothers in the world could have taught her that.

Julius loved the Maya who taught him
that even though he was a pig he didn't
have to act like he lived in a barn.

Julius didn't think all the Alaskan pigs
in the world could have taught him that.

170

Maya shared the things she'd learned
from Julius with her friends.
Swinging . . .
trying on hats, and dancing to jazz records.

Julius shared the things Maya had
taught him with her parents . . . sometimes.

And that was all right, because living
with Maya and sharing everything was even
better than being a cool pig from Alaska.

ANGELA JohnSon

When did you first start writing?

I had a diary when I was in the third grade, and I wrote in it every day. I still have it, so I know what I used to write about— mostly my friends and my family.

What about your writing as you got older?

After college, I wrote a lot of poetry. I used to baby-sit for a writer named Cynthia Rylant. She always had lots of children's books around, so I began reading them. I thought, "Yes, this is it!" I looked at my writing differently, and I knew that I wanted to be a writer.

Dav Pilkey

What made you decide to draw the pictures for *Julius*?

Angie Johnson is a friend of mine, and she asked me to illustrate *Julius*. I had a picture in my mind of what I wanted Maya to look like, but I couldn't quite pin it down. I asked Angie if I could look at her photo album. When I opened the album, I couldn't believe my eyes! There was a picture of Angie as a little girl. She looked just the same as the girl in my mind!

Response Corner

A Book of Good Manners

Julius learns good manners from Maya. Pretend you are Julius and make a book about good manners.

You will need: pig-shaped paper

1. Talk about manners. List some rules for good manners on a chart.

- Eat quietly.
- Use a napkin when you eat.
- Clean up your own mess.
- Hang up your own towel.
- Be quiet when others are reading.
- Do not eat hats.
- Be neat in stores.

2. Write one of the manners rules and draw a picture to go with it.

3. Put everyone's pages together.

After you make your book of manners, you can
- act out the good manners with a partner.
- share your book with another class.

What Do You Think?

Would you like Julius to live with you?
Why or why not?

OUR FAMILY COMES FROM 'ROUND THE WORLD

by Mary Ann Hoberman

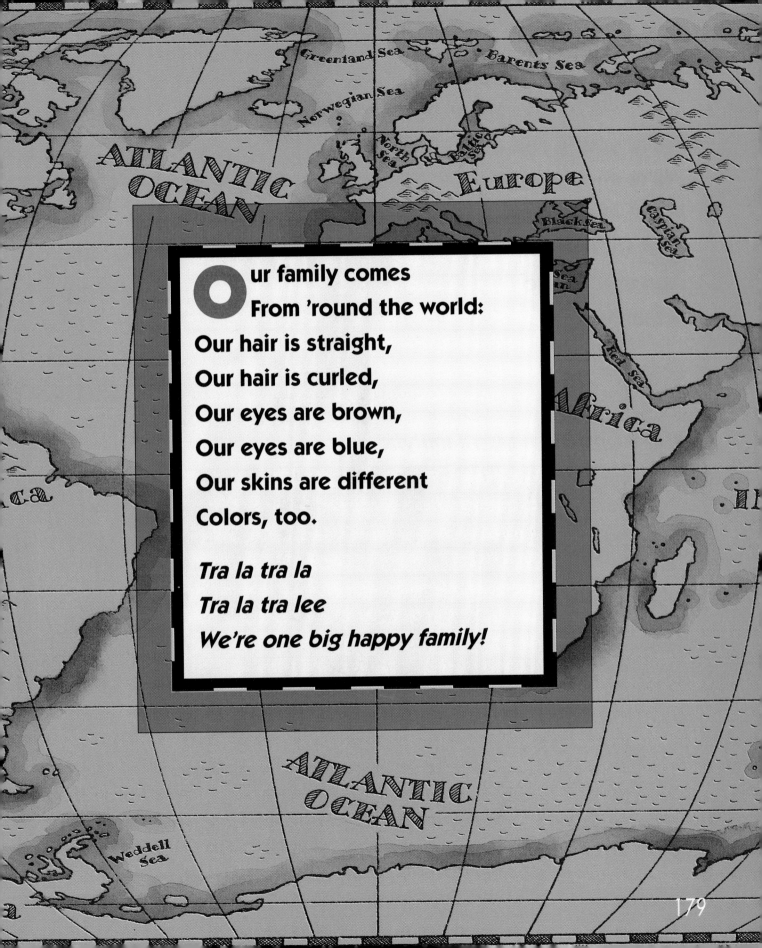

Our family comes
From 'round the world:
Our hair is straight,
Our hair is curled,
Our eyes are brown,
Our eyes are blue,
Our skins are different
Colors, too.

Tra la tra la
Tra la tra lee
We're one big happy family!

We're girls and boys,
We're big and small,
We're young and old,
We're short and tall.
We're everything
That we can be
And still we are
A family.

O la dee da
O la dee dee
We're one big happy family!

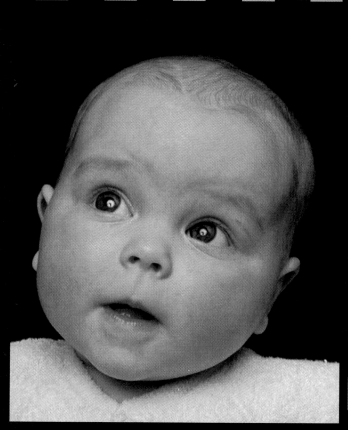

We laugh and cry,
We work and play,
We help each other
Every day.
The world's a lovely
Place to be
Because we are
A family.

Hurray hurrah
Hurrah hurree
We're one big happy family!

New Shoes

Johanna Hurwitz
Illustrated by Jerry Pinkney

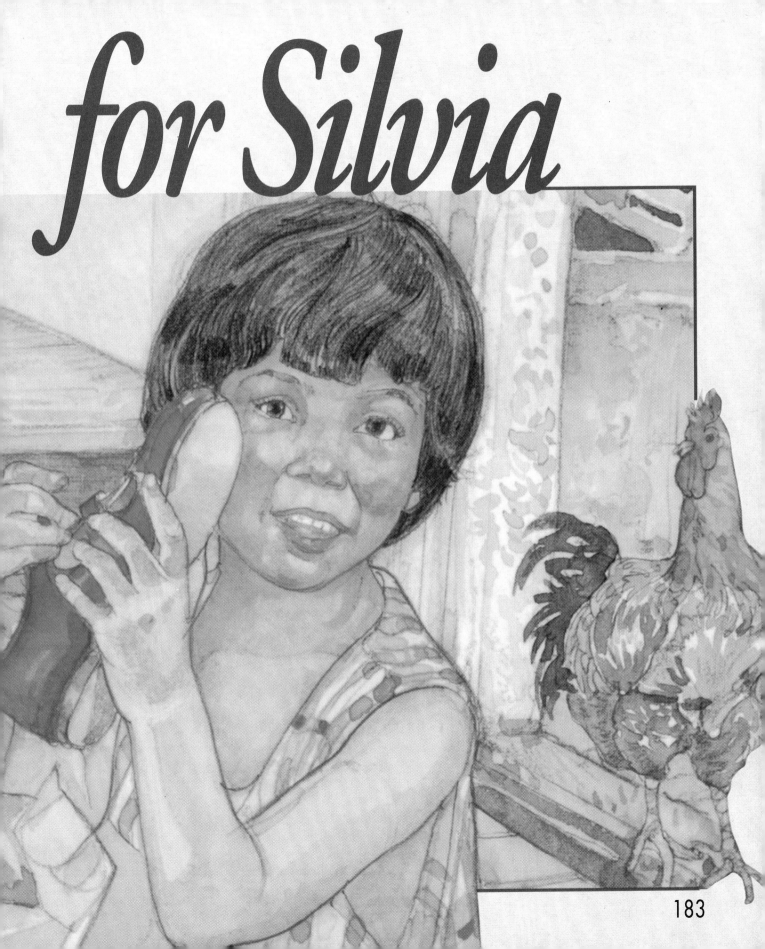

for Silvia

Once, far away in another America,
a package arrived at the post office.
The package came from Tía Rosita.
Inside there were gifts for the whole family.

For Silvia there was a wonderful present—a pair of bright red shoes with little buckles that shone in the sun like silver.

Right away, Silvia took off her old shoes and put on the beautiful new ones. Then she walked around so everyone could see.

"*Mira, mira,*" she called. "Look, look."

"Those shoes are as red as the setting sun," her grandmother said. "But they are too big for you."

"Your shoes are as red as the inside of a watermelon," said Papa. "But they are too big. You will fall if you wear them."

"Tía Rosita has sent you shoes the color of a rose," said Mama. "We will put them away until they fit you."

189

Silvia was sad. What good were new shoes
if she couldn't wear them?

That night she slept with them in her bed.

The next morning Silvia put on the red shoes again.
Perhaps she had grown during the night.

No. The shoes were still too big. But she saw
that they were just the right size to make beds for
two of her dolls. Even though it was morning, the
dolls went right to sleep in their new red beds.

A week passed, and Silvia tried on the red shoes again. Perhaps she had grown during the week.

No. The shoes were still too big. But she saw that they made a fine two-car train. She pushed them all around the floor. What a good ride the babies had in their red train!

Another week passed, and Silvia tried on the red shoes again. Certainly by now she had grown big enough so they would fit.

No. The shoes were still too big. But Silvia
found some string and tied it to the shoes.
Then she pulled the shoes like oxen
working in the field.

Still another week passed, and Silvia tried on the red shoes again. Would they fit now?

No. The shoes were still too big. But she saw that they were just the right size to hold the pretty shells and smooth pebbles that she had collected when she went to the beach with her grandparents.

Another week passed, and another and another. Sometimes Silvia was so busy playing with the other children or helping her mama with the new baby or feeding the chickens or looking for their eggs that she forgot to try on her new red shoes.

One day Mama wrote a letter to Tía Rosita. Silvia thought about the red shoes. She emptied out all the shells and pebbles and dusted the shoes off on her skirt. They were as red and beautiful as ever. Would they fit today?

Yes.

"Mira, mira," she cried, running to show Mama and the baby. "Look, look. My shoes are not too big now."

Silvia wore her new red shoes when she walked to the post office with Mama to mail the letter.

"Maybe there will be a new package for us," said Silvia.

"Packages don't come every day," said Mama.

"Maybe next time Tía Rosita will send me new blue shoes," said Silvia.

They mailed the letter and walked home. Silvia's shoes were as red as the setting sun. They were as red as the inside of a watermelon. They were as red as a rose. The buckles shone in the sun like silver.

And best of all, the shoes were just the right size for Silvia.

203

JOHANNA HURWITZ

Johanna Hurwitz wrote *New Shoes for Silvia* after a visit to Central America. She took a pair of red shoes to the girl in the house where she was staying. The shoes were too big at first, but the girl loved them. She couldn't wait to grow into them. That gave the author her story idea.

"I took lots of pictures while I was visiting," says Johanna Hurwitz. "I gave those pictures to Jerry Pinkney. He used them for his drawings. I wanted the story and the pictures to show the beauty of the country and the warmth of the people."

Johanna Hurwitz

JERRY PINKNEY

Jerry Pinkney used the pictures taken by Johanna Hurwitz to help him paint the pictures for *New Shoes for Silvia*. He says, "The best thing about doing the paintings was learning about the people of Central America. I always like learning something new."

Jerry Pinkney painted Silvia's red shoes many times. "Shoes are hard to paint because they have such an interesting shape. But I always enjoy a challenge!"

Jerry Pinkney

RESPONSE CORNER

A New Gift For Silvia

Silvia's aunt sent her a special
gift. Now it's your turn to
give a gift. You can make a
surprise gift for Silvia and
write clues to help
someone guess
what it is.

1. Fold a sheet of paper in half. Then fold it in half the other way. Color the outside to look like a gift.

2. Unfold the paper and draw a gift. Write the name of the gift.

a basketball

3. Fold the paper and write your clues.

1. It is round and orange.
2. You can throw it.
3. You can play a game with it.
4. A hoop is in the game. What is it?

Later, you can
• trade gifts with a classmate. Read the clues and try to guess what's inside.

What Do You Think?

How did you feel at the end of the story? What made you feel this way?

Glossary

WHAT IS A GLOSSARY?

A glossary is like a small dictionary. This glossary is here to help you. You can look up a word and then read a sentence that uses that word. Some words have a picture to help you.

A

across Go **across** to the other side.

also We went to the library and **also** to the park.

around The dog ran all the way **around** the tree.

B

breakfast

beach It's fun to play at the **beach.**

beaks Birds pecked at seeds with their **beaks.**

been Have you **been** working?

behind Patty is in line **behind** Maria.

breakfast I eat **breakfast** in the morning.

C

cheeks That baby has fat **cheeks.**

children **Children** go to school.

city There are many buildings in a big **city.**

city

dinner

door

eyes

cold   The winter wind is **cold.**

cubes   I put ice **cubes** in my water to make it cold.

D

dinner   My family eats **dinner** together.

done   After the cleaning is **done,** we will have lunch.

door   I opened the **door** and went inside.

E

eyes   I see with my **eyes.**

F

far   I take the bus to school because I live **far** away.

feeding   She is **feeding** the dog a treat.

food   Eating the right **food** helps you grow.

front   The leader is at the **front** of the line.

G

give   Please **give** that book to me.

goldfish   I have a pet **goldfish.**

great   We had a **great** time playing ball.

grew   Emily **grew** tired as the day went on.

H

heat   He felt the **heat** from the fire.

hurry   Will you please **hurry** up so we won't be late?

I

ice   **Ice** helps keep things cold.

L

left   She was cold because she **left** her coat at home.

letter   Billy wrote a **letter** to his grandmother.

M

made   Roger **made** a boat out of paper.

may   You **may** go home when you have finished.

goldfish

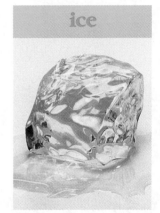

ice

July 10
Dear Grandma,
Please come visit
us soon.
Love, Billy

letter

211

maybe **Maybe** you can come over to my house.

mean What did you **mean** when you said that?

N

never **Never** play in the street!

nice The sun is shining and it is a **nice** day.

O

other The **other** class eats lunch after our class.

outdoors

outdoors We like to play **outdoors** when it's warm.

P

part I liked the funny **part** of the movie best.

please **Please** help me clean up.

pretty I like all the **pretty** colors of the rainbow.

R

rose   A **rose** is a flower.

S

scary   It was **scary** to go on the fast ride.

school   I learn about math at **school.**

screaming   The baby was **screaming** for food.

scrubbed   Dad **scrubbed** the dog with a brush.

seeds   The **seeds** we planted are growing.

shadow   A tree's **shadow** is very long in the morning.

shaking   The puppy was **shaking** because it was cold.

shared   Ron **shared** his lunch with a friend.

rose

seeds

shadow

213

smiled

show   Will you **show** me how you did that trick?

skirt   Shari wore a red **skirt.**

slept   Tara **slept** at her grandma's house.

smiled   The baby **smiled** because she was happy.

snapped   "Be quiet!" she **snapped** at the barking dog.

someone   **Someone** lost a pencil.

something   Did you buy **something** to give Fred for his birthday?

space   The rocket blasted off into outer **space.**

star   I see a very bright **star** in the sky.

started   Trang opened his book and **started** to read.

steps   The **steps** lead up to the front door.

street   The car drove down the **street.**

swing   I like to **swing** up and down.

steps

swing

T

take   Please **take** me with you to the store.

tasted   The food **tasted** very good.

teeth   Bill brushes his **teeth** after he eats.

today   **Today** was my best day in first grade.

took   We **took** off down the road in a hurry.

trapped   She **trapped** the bug in her net.

V

visit   Come to my house and **visit** me soon.

W

wait   Can you **wait** for me at the corner?

week   A **week** has seven days.

tasted

teeth

215

Acknowledgments

For permission to reprint copyrighted material, grateful acknowledgment is made to the following sources:

Candlewick Press, Cambridge, MA: Cover illustration from *You're a Genius, Blackboard Bear* by Martha Alexander. Copyright © 1995 by Martha Alexander.

Coward-McCann, Inc.: Cover illustration from *Millions of Cats* by Wanda Gag. Copyright © 1928 by Coward-McCann, Inc., renewed © 1956 by Robert Janssen.

Dial Books for Young Readers, a division of Penguin Books USA Inc.: From *Spacey Riddles* by Katy Hall and Lisa Eisenberg, illustrated by Simms Taback. Text copyright © 1992 by Katy Hall and Lisa Eisenberg; illustrations copyright © 1992 by Simms Taback. Cover illustration from *What Next, Baby Bear!* by Jill Murphy. Copyright © 1983 by Jill Murphy.

Greenwillow Books, a division of William Morrow & Company, Inc.: *Geraldine's Baby Brother* by Holly Keller. Copyright © 1994 by Holly Keller. Cover illustration from *Furry* by Holly Keller. Copyright © 1992 by Holly Keller.

HarperCollins Publishers: Cover illustration by Melissa Sweet from *Blast Off! Poems About Space*, selected by Lee Bennett Hopkins. Illustration copyright © 1995 by Melissa Sweet. "The New Student" from *The Adventures of Snail at School* by John Stadler. Copyright © 1993 by John Stadler.

Henry Holt and Company, Inc.: "The Stars"/"Las estrellas" from *Grandmother's Nursery Rhymes/Las Nanas de Abuelita* by Nelly Palacio Jaramillo. Text copyright © 1994 by Nelly Palacio Jaramillo.

Lee Bennett Hopkins, on behalf of Prince Redcloud: "Why" by Prince Redcloud.

Dorling Kindersley Limited, London: From *Pets* by Michael Dunning. Copyright © 1991 by Dorling Kindersley Limited, London.

Little, Brown and Company: Cover illustration from *D. W. All Wet* by Marc Brown. Copyright © 1988 by Marc Brown. "Our Family Comes from 'Round the World" from *Fathers, Mothers, Sisters, Brothers: A Collection of Family Poems* by Mary Ann Hoberman. Text copyright © 1991 by Mary Ann Hoberman. "The Dog" from *Custard and Company* by Ogden Nash. Text copyright © 1957 by Ogden Nash; text copyright © renewed 1985 by Frances Nash, Isabel Nash Eberstadt, and Linnel Nash Smith.

Little Simon, an imprint of Simon & Schuster: From *Out In Space* by Tim Wood, illustrated by Tony Wells. Text copyright © 1990 by Tim Wood; illustrations copyright © 1990 by Tony Wells.

Lodestar Books, an affiliate of Dutton Children's Books, a division of Penguin Books USA Inc.: Cover photograph from *See How They Grow: Kitten* by Jane Burton. Copyright © 1991 by Dorling Kindersley Limited, London.

Morrow Junior Books, a division of William Morrow & Company, Inc.: *New Shoes for Silvia* by Johanna Hurwitz, illustrated by Jerry Pinkney. Text copyright © 1993 by Johanna Hurwitz; illustrations copyright © 1993 by Jerry Pinkney.

Orchard Books, New York: *Julius* by Angela Johnson, illustrated by Dav Pilkey. Text copyright © 1993 by Angela Johnson; illustrations copyright © 1993 by Dav Pilkey. Cover illustration by David Soman from *When I Am Old with You* by Angela Johnson. Illustration copyright © 1990 by David Soman.

G. P. Putnam's Sons: "Little" from *Everything and Anything* by Dorothy Aldis. Text copyright 1925-1927; text copyright renewed 1953-1955 by Dorothy Aldis. Cover illustration from *A Mother for Choco* by Keiko Kasza. Copyright © 1992 by Keiko Kasza.

Simon & Schuster Books for Young Readers, a division of Simon & Schuster: *Dreams* by Ezra Jack Keats. Copyright © 1974 by Ezra Jack Keats. Cover illustration from *Pet Show* by Ezra Jack Keats. Copyright © 1972 by Ezra Jack Keats. Cover illustration by Cecily Lang from *Pablo's Tree* by Pat Mora. Illustration copyright © 1994 by Cecily Lang. "The Bath" from *Henry and Mudge in the Green Time* by Cynthia Rylant, illustrated by Suçie Stevenson. Text copyright © 1987 by Cynthia Rylant; illustrations copyright © 1987 by Suçie Stevenson.

Troll Associates: *Planets* by Kim Jackson. Text copyright © 1985 by Troll Associates.

Viking Penguin, a division of Penguin Books USA Inc.: From *I Took My Frog to the Library* by Eric A. Kimmel, illustrated by Blanche Sims. Text copyright © 1990 by Eric A. Kimmel; illustrations copyright © 1990 by Blanche Sims.

Photo Credits

Key: (t) top, (b) bottom, (l) left, (r) right.
Ezra Jack Keats Foundation, 30; Carlo Ontal, 48; Rick Friedman/Black Star/Harcourt Brace & Company, 49, 93; Tom Sobolik/Black Star/Harcourt Brace & Company, 149, 204, 205; Courtesy of Orchard Books, 174, 175; Ron Kunzman/Harcourt Brace & Company, 204-5; Richard Hutchings, 32-33, 70-71, 94-95, 109, 113, 114, 118, 121, 122,176-177; John Johnson, 52-53; Michael Dunning, 54-68; NASA, 74; Courtesy of Hansen Planetarium and Science Source/Photo Researchers 106-111, 114-121, 123; HBJ photo, 111; Harcourt Brace photo, 116; Giraudon/Art Resource, 124-125; Photos from Cynthia Rylant's autobiography "Best Wishes" copyright © 1992 published by Richard C. Owens Publishers, Inc.; Lawrence Migdale (tl), 178; (tl), 181; Shelley Rotner Photography (tr), (br), 178; Myrleen Ferguson Cate/PhotoEdit (bl), 178; The Photographers' Library/Uniphoto (tr), 180; Paul Barton/The Stock Market (bl), (br), 180; Robert Brenner/PhotoEdit (tr), 181; Ariel Skelley/The Stock Market (bl), 181.

Illustration Credits

Richard Bernal, Cover Art, 1, 2; Jennifer Beck Harris, 4-5, 10-13; Mercedes Macdonald, 6-7, 72-75; Nancy Davis, 8-9, 130-133; Ezra Jack Keats, 14-31; Suçie Stevenson, 34-49; John Kanzler, 50-51; John Stadler, 76-93; Tony Wells, 96-101; Scott Sheidly, 102; Simms Taback,103-105; Brian Dugan, 106-107;Scott Sheidly, 112-113; Peggy Tagel, 126-127; Clarence Porter, 128-129; Holly Keller, 134-149; Rita Lascaro, 150-151; Greta Buchart, 152-153; Dav Pilkey, 154-175; Holly Cooper, 178-181, 206-207; Jerry Pinkney, 182-205.